NUMBER THE

by
Lois Lowry

Student Packet

Written by
Phyllis A. Green

Contains masters for:

	1	Anticipation Guide
	1	Study Guide (8 pages)
	1	Vocabulary Activity
	1	Location Chart
	1	Literary Devices
	1	Characters
	1	Thesaurus
	1	Writing
	1	Writer's Craft
	1	Sociogram
	1	Visualization
	1	Book's Themes
	1	Award-Winning Books
	1	Historical Fiction—Analysis
	3	Comprehension Quizzes
	1	Final Examination
PLUS		Detailed Answer Key

Note

The text used to prepare this guide was the Dell Yearling paperback edition. The page references may differ in other editions.

Please note: Please assess the appropriateness of this book for the age level and maturity of your students prior to reading and discussing it with your class.

ISBN 1-56137-605-1

To order, contact your local school supply store, or—

Novel Units, Inc.
P.O. Box 97
Bulverde, TX 78163-0097

Web site: www.educyberstor.com

Name________________________________

Number the Stars
Activity #1: Anticipation Guide
Use Before Reading

Anticipation Guide

Directions: Respond to the following eight statements by indicating "agree" or "disagree" prior to reading the book. The statements refer to themes and ideas raised in the book. After reading the book, again indicate "agree" or "disagree." If you changed your opinion or intensified it, explain in a sentence or two on the reverse side of this sheet.

	Before Reading	After Reading
1. Friends are all-important—any sacrifice or hardship in the name of friendship is warranted.	________	________
2. Only adults and near-adults are responsible enough to carry out vital tasks.	________	________
3. The governmental authority should be followed without question.	________	________
4. There are important lessons to be learned from the Holocaust.	________	________
5. Reading historical fiction is an intriguing way to learn the lessons of history.	________	________
6. Heroes come in many sizes and shapes.	________	________
7. Lying or telling falsehoods or omitting details is never justified.	________	________
8. Bravery is knowing what you need to do, staying focused, and overcoming your fears.	________	________

Name_______________________________

Study Guide

Directions: These questions are to help you note the details and important themes in the book as well as the writer's craft in creating the book. Your teacher will direct you in recording answers—mentally, in written notes ready for oral discussion, or more formally. Some students find it helpful to review the questions before reading a chapter.

Chapter 1, "Why Are You Running?" — Pages 1-10

1. How does the author grab your attention at the start of the first chapter?

2. What is the setting (time and place) of the novel? How do you know?

3. What was the encounter with the German soldiers? Why were the girls scared?

4. Why do Ellen and Annemarie decide not to tell their mothers about the soldiers?

5. What is the mood of the chapter?

Chapter 2, "Who Is the Man Who Rides Past?" — Pages 11-17

1. Explain the chapter title.

2. Why did Christian X feel safe riding his horse Jubilee through the German soldiers on the streets of Copenhagen?

3. Why did Christian X surrender to the Germans so quickly?

4. What happened to Lise?

Chapter 3, "Where Is Mrs. Hirsch?" — Pages 18-26

1. How did life change in occupied Denmark?

2. Why is the button shop important in the story?

3. How can the Danes be bodyguards?

4. Why did Peter arrive after the curfew?

5. Why did the Germans impose a curfew?

Chapter 4, "It Will Be a Long Night" — Pages 27-38

1. What are the fish shoes?

2. What were the "fireworks" on Kirsti's birthday?

3. Why does Mr. Johansen once again have three daughters at the end of the chapter?

Chapter 5, "Who Is the Dark-Haired One?" — Pages 39-49

1. How do Ellen and Annemarie act when they go to bed?

2. How do the soldiers treat the Johansens' at 4 a.m.?

3. Why does Annemarie hold the Star of David so tightly?

Chapter 6, "Is the Weather Good for Fishing?" — Pages 50-59

1. Why did Mama and Papa disagree in this chapter?

2. Why did Papa talk of bringing cigarettes to Uncle Henrik when there were no cigarettes in the stores?

3. How does Kirsti worry Mama and Annemarie?

4. Where is Gilleleje?

Chapter 7, "The House by the Sea" — Pages 60-66

1. How does the author express a look with "fresh eyes" at the start of the chapter?

2. What was Mama's warning? Was it justified?

3. What contrasts does the author suggest in this chapter?

Chapter 8, "There Has Been a Death" — Pages 67-73

1. What is Annemarie's joke about the butter? Why do Mama and Ellen laugh?

2. How do Mama, Ellen, Annemarie, and Kirsti occupy themselves while visiting Henrik?

3. What explanations and comments from adults seem mysterious and strange to Annemarie?

Chapter 9, "Why Are You Lying?" — Pages 74-81

1. How does Uncle Henrik answer Annemarie's accusation that he and Mama are lying to her?

2. Why does the family stage the mourning of Great-aunt Birte?

3. Who reappears at the end of Chapter 9?

Chapter 10, "Let Us Open the Casket" — Pages 82-87

1. Who pounded on the cottage door in the night?

2. How do Annemarie and Mama display their bravery?

3. What is revealed in the psalm Peter reads aloud?

Chapter 11, "Will We See You Again Soon, Peter?" — Pages 88-94

1. What is found when the casket is opened?

2. What is Peter's role in the proceedings?

3. How do the Rosens change their sources of pride as they entrust themselves to Peter and Henrik?

4. What do you think the important packet for Henrik is?

Chapter 12, "Where Was Mama?" — Pages 95-100

1. What is Mama's task in Chapter 12? What makes it difficult?

2. How do Ellen and Annemarie say good-bye?

3. Why does Annemarie go in search of her mother?

4. How does the chapter end?

Chapter 13, "Run! As Fast As You Can!" — Pages 101-105

1. What had happened to Mama?

2. What disturbs Mama and Annemarie when they find the packet for Uncle Henrik?

3. How do Annemarie and Mama hope to "save the day?"

4. What is in the packet for Uncle Henrik?

Chapter 14, "On the Dark Path" — Pages 106-112

1. Why is it uncomfortable as Annemarie hurries to take the packet to Uncle Henrik?

2. What does Annemarie think about as she runs to Uncle Henrik's boat?

3. What is the real growl Annemarie hears at the end of the chapter?

Chapter 15, "My Dogs Smell Meat!" — Pages 113-119

1. How does Annemarie follow Mama's advice in dealing with the soldiers?

2. How does Annemarie distract the soldiers?

3. How do both Annemarie and the soldiers show displeasure with each other?

4. Why does Uncle Henrik say he hopes the soldiers choke on his bread?

Chapter 16, "I Will Tell You Just a Little" — Pages 120-127

1. How can you tell the climax of the book has passed?

2. Why does Uncle Henrik suggest the milking lesson?

3. What explanations does Annemarie get as to the events at the farm?

Chapter 17, "All This Long Time" — Pages 128-132

1. How do the Johansens and other characters in the book fare after the Rosens flee?

2. How does Lowry end the book?

Afterword — Pages 133-137

1. What answers does Lowry provide in her Afterword?

2. What information about historical fiction does Lowry provide in the Afterword?

Name______________________________

Vocabulary Scramble

Directions: Look over these identified vocabulary words, listed chapter-by-chapter. Identify nouns, verbs, and adjectives with different colors of highlighter or other mark. Choose words for the word maps.

Chapter 1
lanky rucksack plodding
contempt sneering obstinate
hoodlums sabotage impassive

Chapter 2
trousseau intricate

Chapter 3
rationed haughtily sarcastically
swastika curfew

Chapter 4
sophisticated exasperated
belligerently ablaze submerged
tense dismay dubiously tension

Chapter 5
imperious intoned stalk

Chapter 6
tentatively mourning
sprawling massive
exasperation pranced

Chapter 7
awe gnarled appliquéd

Chapter 8
haze ruefully
specter gesturing

Name______________________________

Chapter 9
deftly dismayed cocked hearse
wryly trudged wail urgency

Chapter 10
surge staccato
condescending strode

Chapter 11
protruding commotion
misshapen

Chapter 13
faltered winced sprawling

Chapter 14
donned peered latticed
populated vivid wriggle segment
brusque prolong tantalize taut

Chapter 15
enrage consumed withering
insolently caustic subsided strident

Chapter 16
warily confronting

Chapter 17
devastating bleak

Afterword
deprivation integrity compassion
permeated orchestrated sabotage

Name________________________________

Word Map for a Noun

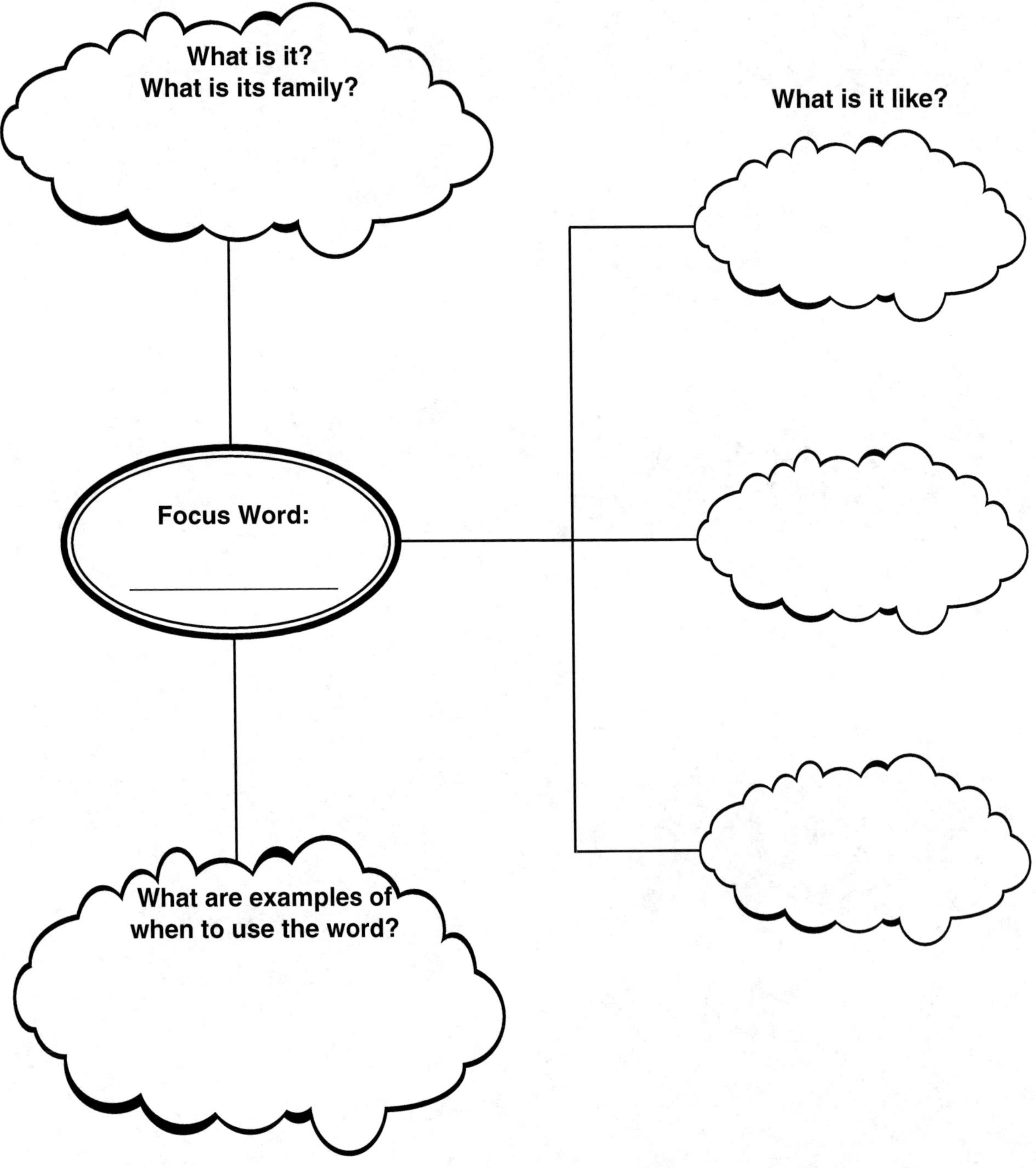

Name________________________________

Word Map for a Verb

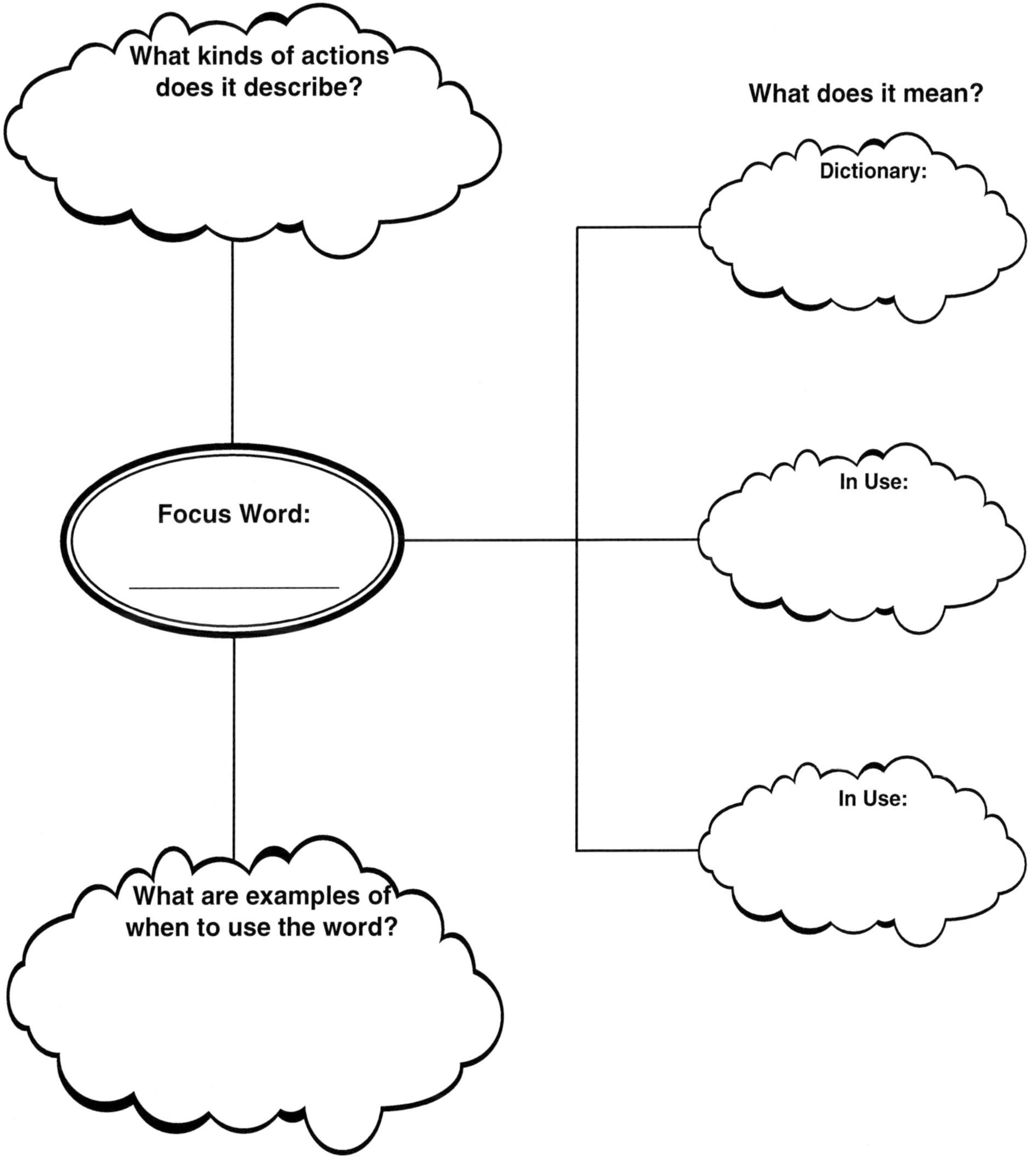

Name______________________________

Word Map for an Adjective

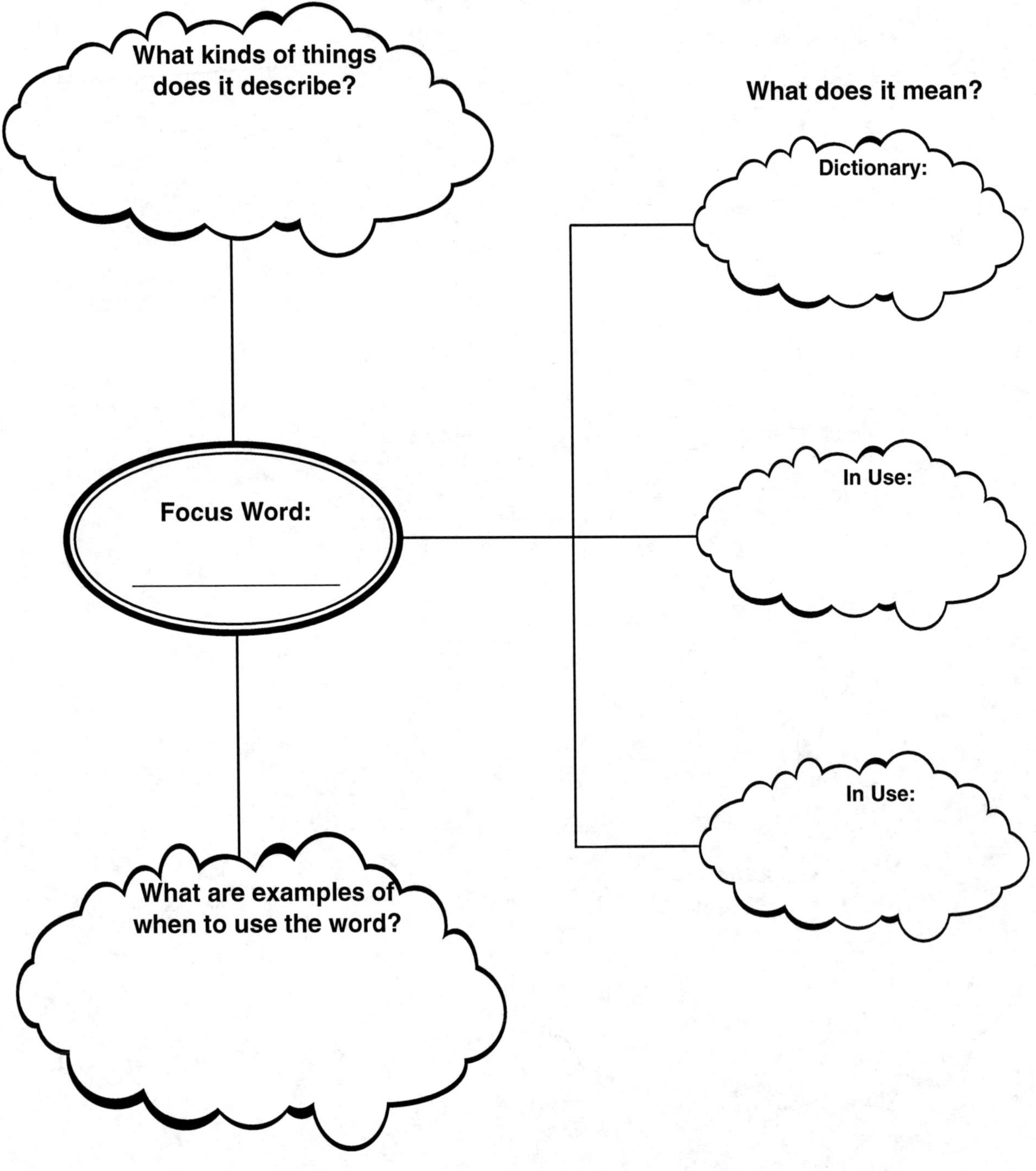

Name______________________________

Map of Denmark and Surrounding Areas

Directions: Locate the places mentioned in the book.

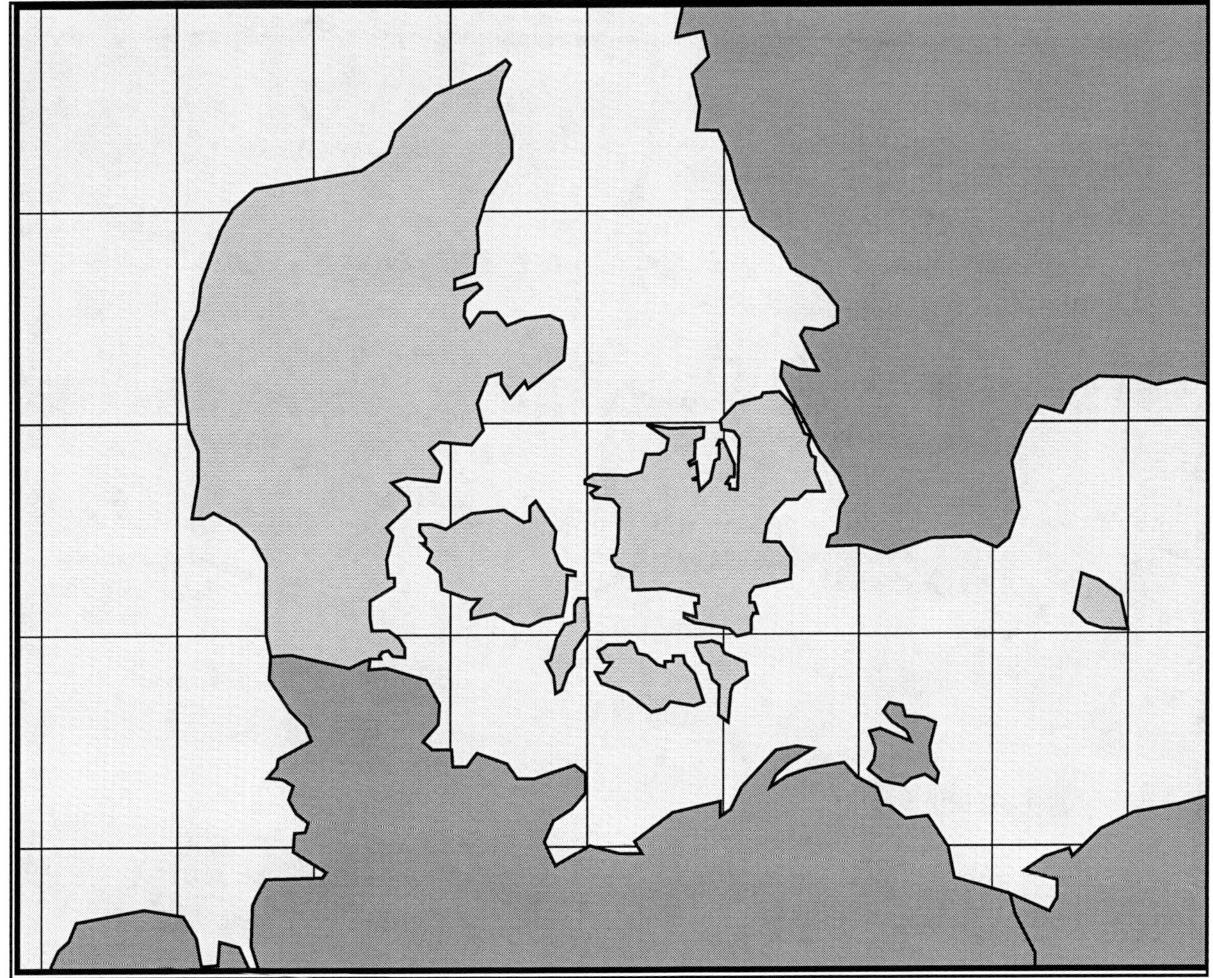

Name________________________

Literary Devices From the Book

Directions: Locate each device mentioned below and answer the questions posed.

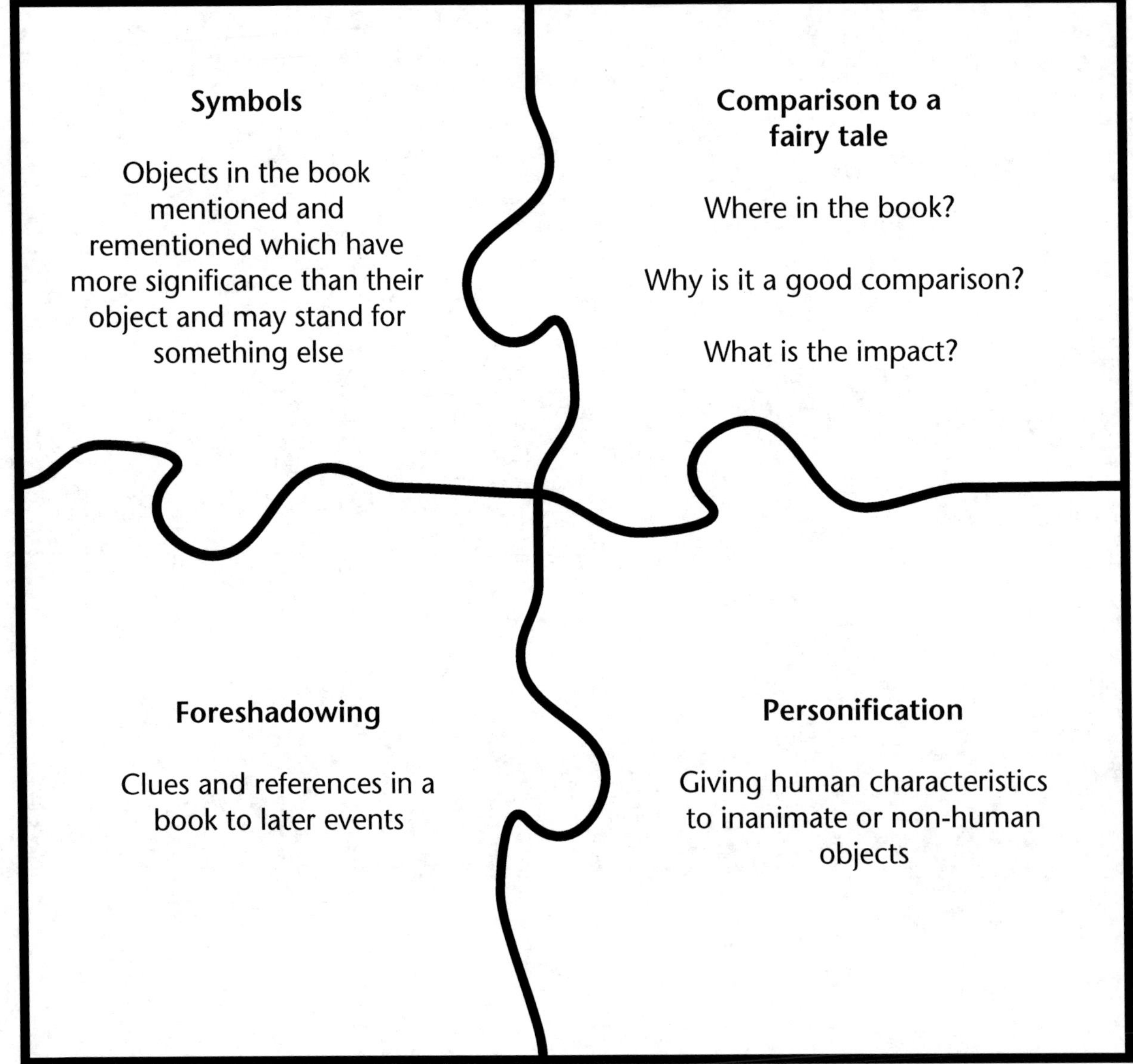

Name________________________________

Character Poems

Directions: Choose a poem type to write about your favorite character from the book.

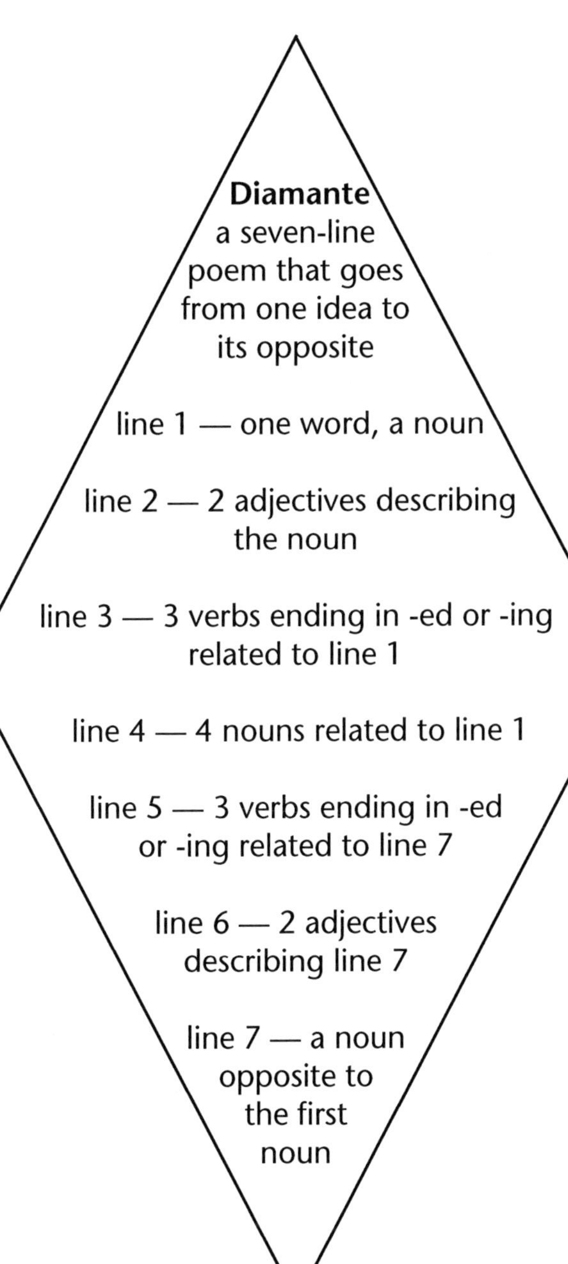

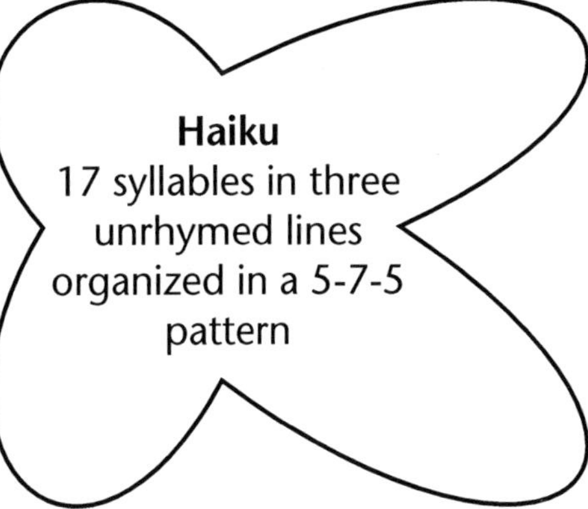

Limerick
5 lines — first, second, and fifth lines rhyme and contain 3 accented syllables. Lines 3 and 4 rhyme and contain 2 accented syllables.

Cinquain
5 line poem, unrhymed.
Line 1 has 2 syllables;
line 2 has 4 syllables;
line 3 has 6 syllables;
line 4 has 8 syllables;
line 5 has 2 syllables.

Name______________________________

Diamante

____

____________ ____________

____________ ____________ ____________

____________ ____________ ____________ ____________

____________ ____________ ____________

____________ ____________

____

Limerick

____

____

____

____

____

Haiku

____

____

____

Cinquain

____

____

____

____

____

Name______________________________

Thesaurus

Directions: Use a thesaurus to find alternatives to these overused words.

Walk	**Talk**	**Feel**

Say	**Write**	**Know**

Journal Prompts

- What does the book's cover say to you?
- What would be rationed today if there were shortages?
- Why do authors use chapter titles? (Think of examples of memorable chapter titles as well as some good books without chapter titles.)
- What is bravery?
- What are the sources of pride for the characters in the book?
- What are your sources of pride?
- Ellen promises to return to Annemarie. Will she keep her promise? Why or why not?
- What is a hero?
- What does friendship mean to the characters in the book?

Name_______________________________

The Writer's Craft: How does an author choose the words to end each chapter?

Directions: Look back over the ends of the chapters. What do you expect to find?

What is the last sentence from each chapter?

Chapter 1

2

3

4

5

6

7

8

9

10

11

12

13

14

15

16

17

What kind of sentences does Lowry choose to end her chapters?

____

____

____ .

How do the final sentences make you as a reader feel? ______________________

____

____ .

Name________________________________

Annemarie and the Other Characters in the Book

Directions: As the main character, Annemarie interacts with the other characters in various ways. Record these relationships on the sociogram charting below. On each line (remember relationships go two ways), choose a word or phrase to describe the relationship.

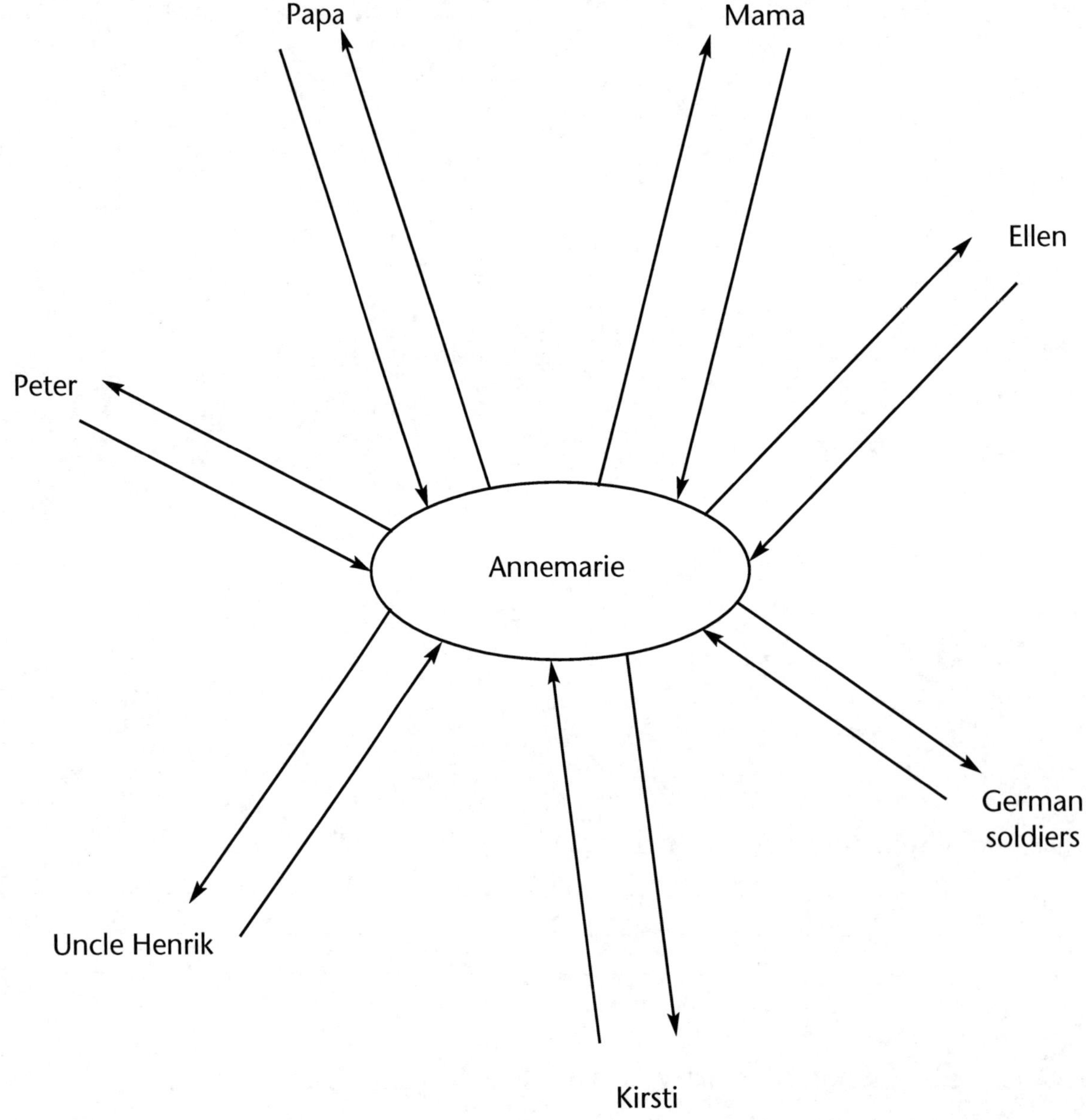

Name________________________________

Picturing the Characters

Directions: You will need several magazines for this activity. Picture these characters in your mind. Then look through the magazines for a picture to use for each character. Choose a representative line from that character to write on a label to attach to the pictures you've chosen.

Annemarie

Ellen

Peter

Mama

Papa

Kirsti

Uncle Henrik

Name________________________________

Create a Word Map For One of the Book's Themes

Directions: Choose one of these themes from the book to be the focus of your word map (bravery, loyalty, friendship, or an idea of your own). Complete a web and then fill in the stars.

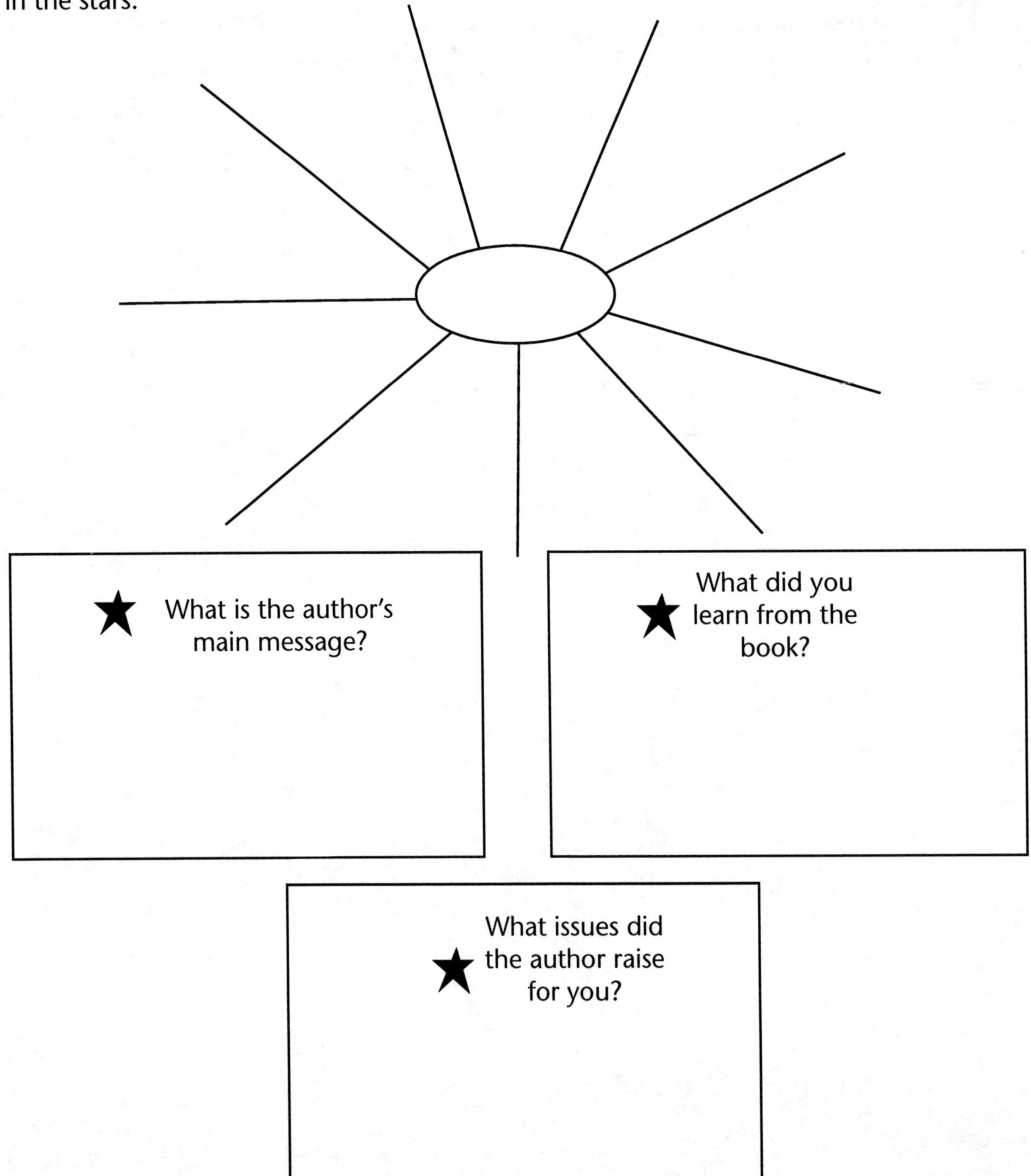

Name________________________________

Investigating Award-Winning Books

The Newbery Medal, named for eighteenth-century British bookseller John Newbery, is awarded annually by the Association for Library Service to Children, a division of the American Library Association, to the author of the most distinguished contribution of American literature for children.

Look at these Newbery winners in recent years:

The Giver
Missing May
Shiloh
Maniac Magee
Number the Stars
Joyful Noise: Poems for Two Voices
Lincoln: A Photobiography
The Whipping Boy
Sarah, Plain and Tall
The Hero and the Crown

Mark those you've read.

Brainstorm a list of descriptive words and phrases you can use for the Newbery books.

Why is *Number the Stars* a book worthy of the award?

____
____
____
____
____
____
____
____
____

Name____________________________

What is Historical Fiction?

What are some books of historical fiction you've read?

What makes these books special? Unique?

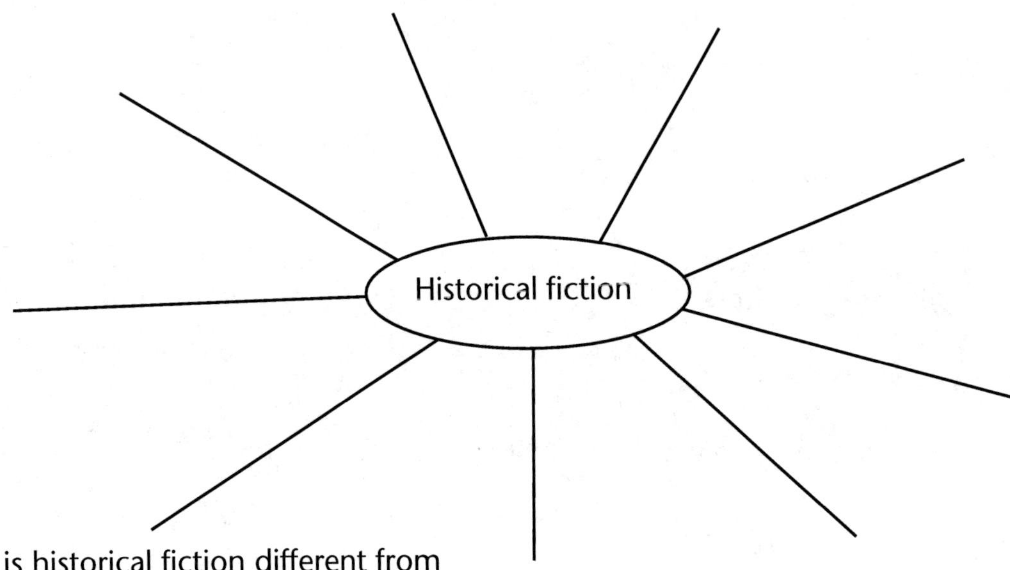

How is historical fiction different from

fiction? ____________________
nonfiction? ____________________
poetry? ____________________
biography? ____________________
fantasy? ____________________
folk tales? ____________________

Prepare a comprehensive definition of historical fiction to remember:

____
____
____
____
____

Name________________________________

Quiz #1

Part I — Fill in the chart to summarize the basic set-up of the story.

Setting (Time and Place)	
Characters (name 6)	
Conflict	
Point-of-View	

Part II — Choose 3 of the details from the book to identify in a short sentence.

broken button
seashells
Gone With the Wind
Jubilee
Tivoli Gardens
Ellen's necklace
fish shoes

1. ____________________
2. ____________________
3. ____________________

Part III — In a short paragraph, make predictions about the rest of the book.

____

Name______________________________

Number the Stars
Quiz II — Page 1
After Chapter 10

Quiz #2

Part I — Select 5 important happenings from the story to put into this flow chart. Be sure to choose carefully so that you'll cover the plot in the book through Chapter 10.

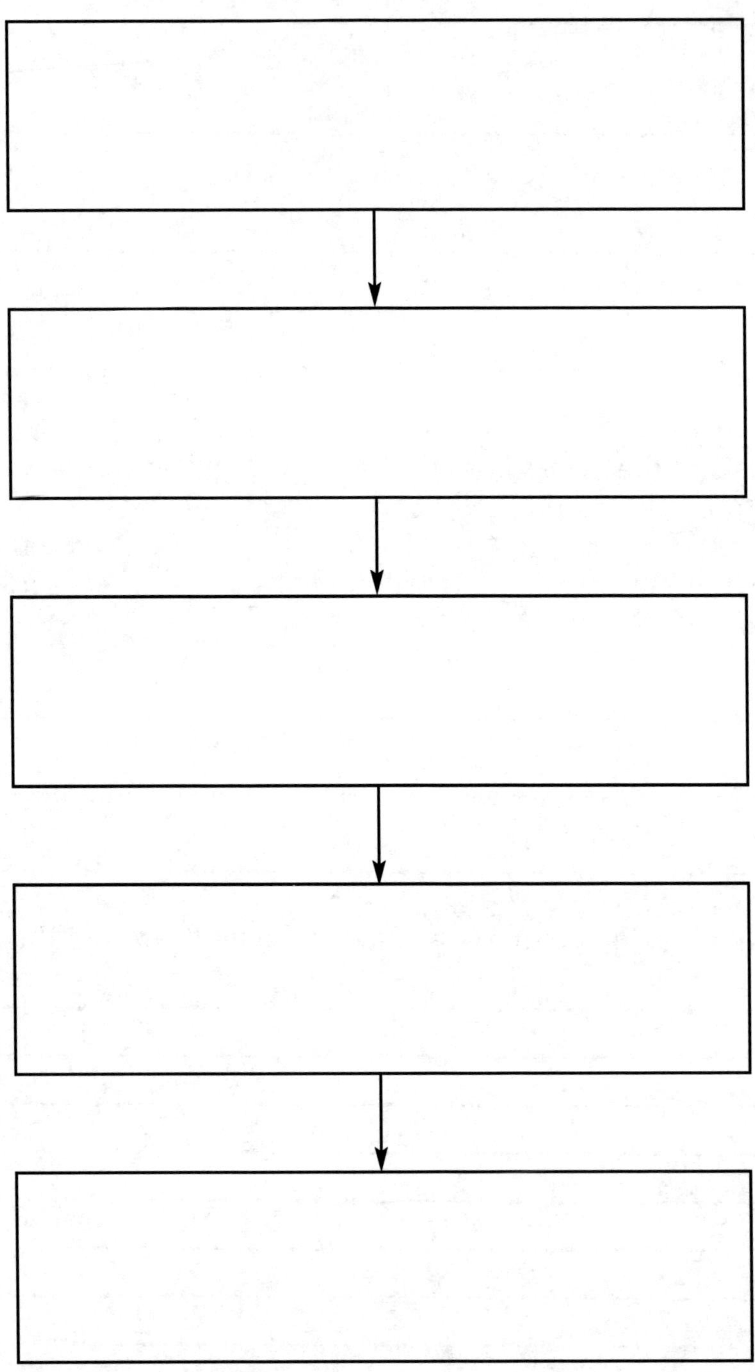

Name______________________________

Part II — Choose five of the following words to use in a sentence. Be sure your sentences will display your understanding of the words.

tentatively	haze	urgency
massive	gesturing	cocked
mourning	ruefully	trudged
exasperated	specter	surge
sprawling	deftly	staccato
pranced	hearse	condescending
awe	wail	strode
gnarled	dismayed	appliquéd
wryly		

1. ______________________________
2. ______________________________
3. ______________________________
4. ______________________________
5. ______________________________

Part III — Identify these details from the book.

cigarettes ______________________________

Thor ______________________________

Birte ______________________________

Blossom ______________________________

Name______________________________

Quiz #3

Part I — Identify these important details from the book.

packet ______________________________

moonless night ______________________________

tree roots ______________________________

forgotten lunch ______________________________

Little Red Riding-Hood ______________________________

Halte ______________________________

Part II — What was the climax in this part of the book? Answer in a short paragraph.

____

Part III — Match these words with a definition.

___ 1. protruding
___ 2. faltered
___ 3. winced
___ 4. donned
___ 5. brusque
___ 6. caustic
___ 7. enrage
___ 8. tantalize

A. dressed in
B. severely critical
C. bulging
D. anger
E. torment
F. flinched
G. wavered
H. abrupt

Name________________________________

Final Examination

Part I — Match these numbered characters, events, details, and vocabulary words with an appropriate lettered response.

___ 1. Ellen Rosen	A. abrupt
___ 2. Annemarie Johansen	B. doubtfully
___ 3. Kirsti Johansen	C. book character for play
___ 4. Lise Johansen	D. wonder
___ 5. Peter	E. contemptuously
___ 6. Uncle Henrik	F. non-existent
___ 7. Christian X	G. having a grille work
___ 8. Mrs. Hirsch	H. father is a teacher
___ 9. casket	I. is the middle child
___ 10. handkerchief	J. sells buttons
___ 11. Star of David	K. in the Resistance
___ 12. Scarlett O'Hara	L. Rides Jubilee in Copenhagen
___ 13. Great-aunt Birte	M. dolefully
___ 14. rucksack	N. clothes for a bride
___ 15. impassive	O. fisherman
___ 16. trousseau	P. distracts dogs
___ 17. dubiously	Q. holds blankets and jackets
___ 18. awe	R. Jewish symbol
___ 19. ruefully	S. names the kitten
___ 20. insolently	T. emotionless
___ 21. brusque	U. knapsack
___ 22. latticed	V. dies in an auto accident

Name______________________________

Part II — Choose four of these words to use in sentences. Be sure your sentences reveal your understanding of the words.

withering	staccato	insolently
strident	misshapen	vivid
deftly	taut	specter
tantalize	intoned	

1. ____
____
2. ____
____
3. ____
____
4. ____
____

Part III — Choose the most appropriate response to finish each sentence below.

1. *Number the Stars* is

   a. an old favorite which your parents probably read in school
   b. a Caldecott winner
   c. a Newbery winner
   d. a fantasy

2. Lois Lowry is

   a. the main character in the book
   b. the button store owner
   c. the author
   d. the book's editor

3. *Number the Stars* is set

   a. in Denmark
   b. in Germany
   c. in Southwestern U.S.
   d. in an Alaskan fishing village

4. The German soldiers in the beginning of the book

   a. are reminded of their own children when they talk to Kirsti
   b. keep to themselves
   c. patrol the harbors very carefully
   d. resent the assignment out of Germany

5. You know Peter is in the Resistance because

   a. he tells the family openly
   b. he wears a Resistance badge
   c. he recruits others to the cause
   d. he brings the Resistance newspaper and comes to visit at night

6. Lise's trousseau is in a trunk which

   a. provides a fun play chest for Annemarie, Ellen, and Kirsti
   b. hides Ellen's Star of David
   c. is used as an end table
   d. has leather tooling as decoration

7. Papa does not go to Uncle Henrik's with the girls because

   a. he and Henrik have argued
   b. he doesn't want to draw attention to the journey
   c. he has responsibilities at work
   d. he is taken ill at the last minute

8. All of the following are examples of misrepresentation (or lying) in the book except

   a. Great-aunt Birte's funeral
   b. Uncle Henrik's lunch
   c. the three Johansen daughters
   d. the directions given to the soldiers

Name_______________________________

9. The God of Thunder is

   a. the name of the Copenhagen Ferris wheel at Tivoli Gardens
   b. a kitten
   c. Uncle Henrik's boat
   d. Kirsti's favorite book

10. The handkerchief is important in the book because

   a. it hid the packet
   b. it illustrated Mr. Rosen's clumsiness
   c. it misled the dogs
   d. it provided the climax of the plot

Part IV — Choose one of the following themes to use as the basis for a paragraph. In the paragraph use incidents and messages from the book to support your ideas.

bravery   fear   war   resistance   prejudice   opposition

____
____
____
____
____
____
____
____
____
____
____
____
____
____
____
____
____
____

Literary Devices

The fairy tale comparison is in Chapter 2 and again in Chapter 14.
Foreshadowing is seen in Annemarie and courage on page 26 and again in Chapter 8.
Symbols include the Star of David and Christian X.
Personification is found on page 56.

Quiz 1

Part I

Setting — World War II in Denmark
Main Characters — Annemarie Johansen, Mrs. Johansen, Kirsti Johansen, Ellen Rosen, Mrs. Rosen, Peter
Conflict — survival of the Rosens and other Jews in Denmark
Point-of-view — third person

Part II

broken button — on Kirsti's jacket, led the girls to find Mrs. Hirsch's store closed
seashells — presents from Peter for the girls
fish shoes — Kirsti's new shoes of fish skin
Jubilee — Christian X's horse
Tivoli Gardens — amusement park in Copenhagen
Gone with the Wind — popular book which Ellen and Annemarie act out
Ellen's necklace — Star of David, a Jewish symbol

Quiz 2

Part I

Answers vary; look for reasonable choice of the incidents so that taken together they tell the story. German occupation of Denmark — notice for relocation of Jews — Johansens shelter Ellen — girls and Mama flee to Uncle Henrik's — family stages a wake

Part III

cigarettes — long unavailable, some kind of code in phone conversation
Thor — Kirsti's name for the little kitten
Birte — fictitious deceased great-aunt
Blossom — Henrik's cow

Quiz 3

Part I

packet — important to be given to Uncle Henrik
moonless night — makes sneaking to the boat less noticeable, also makes trip harder
tree roots — dangers on the path
forgotten lunch — cover for Annemarie taking packet to Henrik
Little Red Riding-Hood — story Annemarie told herself as she ran through the woods
Halte — what the soldiers had said to stop Annemarie in the beginning of the book

Part II

Annemarie stopped in the woods by soldiers.

Part III

1. C	3. F	5. H	7. D
2. G	4. A	6. B	8. E

Final Examination

Part I

1. H	7. L	13. F	18. D
2. I	8. J	14. U	19. M
3. S	9. Q	15. T	20. E
4. V	10. P	16. N	21. A
5. K	11. R	17. B	22. G
6. O	12. C		

Part III

1. C	4. A	7. B	9. B
2. C	5. D	8. D	10. D
3. A	6. B		

(For answer 10, note that prompt C is also true but not the best response.)

Part IV — See rubric, page 43.

Study Guide

Chapter 1

1. Just starts into a dialogue between 2 school girls — no setting or details revealed yet.
2. Occupied Denmark during World War II. Place names in the book and references to Nazis.
3. Two soldiers with rifles stopped the girls who were running. After answering questions, the girls were told to go home but don't run.
4. don't want to upset mothers
5. ominous, less than happy, wary

Chapter 2

1. The Danish king, Christian X, rode daily on the streets of Copenhagen as a symbol and encouragement to his people.
2. He was well-known and liked by the Danish people, any of whom would protect him if needed.
3. He believed his small army unable to resist and wanted to prevent needless killing.
4. She dies in an accident two weeks before her wedding.

Chapter 3

1. rationing of electricity, sugar; German soldiers, curfew, closing of Jewish shops
2. Annemarie and Ellen find the button shop owned by an old Jewish woman closed and a sign in German on the door. Introduces concern for all Jews in Denmark.
3. Each Dane would protect and shelter Jewish neighbors.
4. Author doesn't say directly but the reader may surmise he's part of the Danish Resistance.
5. to control the people

Chapter 4

1. Kirsti's new shoes are made of fish skin because there is no leather available.
2. Christian X blowing up his naval fleet so the Germans couldn't take them over.
3. The Rosens have fled and Ellen is being hidden with the Johansens. They fear German "relocation."

Chapter 5

1. apprehensive but assured of parental protection
2. impolitely, brusquely, rudely
3. She is fearful of the soldiers finding it.

Chapter 6

1. Different ideas of the safest way to go to Uncle Henrik's without alerting the German soldiers about Ellen Rosen
2. He was talking in code — referring to Ellen.
3. All worry that Kirsti, young, unafraid and outgoing, will reveal information about Ellen Rosen.
4. on the seacoast

Chapter 7

1. Ellen is in awe of the beautiful scenery, the open sea, the birds, a stray kitten.
2. to avoid anyone else lest they not be able to explain Ellen's presence
3. Ellen and Annemarie and their views of Henrik's home; overheard adult conversation now and from Annemarie's memory; anticipated evening meal and fare in Copenhagen; free Denmark and occupied Denmark

Chapter 8

1. That the German soldiers would relocate the butter. The others laugh because of the joke about a sad undesirable state of affairs.
2. visit the cow and pasture, play with the kitten, clean and dust the cottage
3. the talk of grieving Great-aunt Birte and comments about good days for fishing

Chapter 9

1. He explains to Annemarie that the adults are shielding her so she doesn't know too much and will find it easier to be brave.
2. Author doesn't answer directly but the lie is used to explain people coming to the house.
3. Ellen's parents and Peter

Chapter 10

1. German soldiers checking on the people at the cottage
2. Annemarie answers naming the deceased. Mama diverts the soldiers from opening the casket by saying that the body is contaminated with typhus and they've been advised to close the casket.
3. the title of the book

Chapter 11

1. blankets and clothing
2. He seems to be "in charge."
3. They give up candlesticks, books, dreams of the theater, tidy appearance.
4. The author does not reveal, only to emphasize the importance.

Chapter 12

1. To lead the Rosens to Henrik's boat. The path is bumpy and the night is dark.
2. Hug and Ellen promises to return.
3. She awakens at first light and realizes Mama isn't home yet.
4. Annemarie finds Mama on the ground.

Chapter 13

1. She tripped on a root and hurt her ankle. She had to crawl home.
2. The packet must be very important, judging from Peter's care with it.
3. Annemarie will run to the boat with the packet hidden in a lunch basket.
4. The author doesn't reveal. Annemarie asks but Mama doesn't answer.

Chapter 14

1. cold, damp, dark
2. a fairy tale she often told to Kirsti
3. the German soldiers' dogs

Chapter 15

1. She acts as a silly little girl. She thinks how Kirsti would answer each soldier's inquiry.
2. crying
3. Annemarie answers back about the meat. The soldiers sneer at the food and make fun of the handkerchief.
4. He despises the German occupation soldiers.

Chapter 16

1. The mood has changed from anticipation and fear to calm, quiet, and lightness.
2. So he can have a few private moments to explain to Annemarie about the resistance.
3. Peter is part of the Danish Resistance which used fishing boats to smuggle Danish Jews to safety in Sweden. The packet contained a specially prepared handkerchief which threw the dogs into confusion.

Chapter 17

1. The war and shortage and indignities of German occupiers continue. The Danes care for the empty Jewish apartments. Peter is executed.
2. Papa agrees to repair Ellen's Star of David and Annemarie decides to wear it until Ellen returns.

Afterword

1. Where she got her material and ideas for the book, which characters were real, the handkerchief details.
2. The blend of real and imaginary elements in the story, the grounding in factual material.

Essay Evaluation Form

1. **Focus:** Student writes a clear thesis and includes it in the opening paragraph.	10	8	4
2. **Organization:** The final draft reflects the assigned outline; transitions are used to link ideas.	20	16	12
3. **Support:** Adequate quotes are provided and are properly documented.	12	10	7
4. **Detail:** Each quote is explained (as if the teacher had not read the book); ideas are not redundant.	12	10	7
5. **Mechanics:** Spelling, capitalization, and usage are correct.	16	12	8
6. **Sentence Structure:** The student avoids run-ons and sentence fragments.	10	8	4
7. **Verb:** All verbs are in the correct tense; sections in which plot is summarized are in the present tense.	10	8	4
8. Total effect of the essay.	10	8	4
	100	80	50

Comments:

Total: __________

(This rubric may be altered to fit the needs of a particular class. You may wish to show it to students before they write their essays. They can use it as a self-evaluation tool, and they will be aware of exactly how their essays will be graded.)

Notes